AMAZING MILITARY MACHINES

AIR FORCE ONE

BY ELEANOR BRADSHAW

Enslow PUBLISHING

Please visit our website, www.enslow.com. For a free color catalog of all our high-quality books, call toll free 1-800-398-2504 or fax 1-877-980-4454.

Library of Congress Cataloging-in-Publication Data
Names: Bradshaw, Eleanor, author.
Title: Air Force One / Eleanor Bradshaw.
Description: Buffalo, New York : Enslow Publishing, [2025] | Series: Amazing military machines | Includes index.
Identifiers: LCCN 2023059777 | ISBN 9781978539563 (library binding) | ISBN 9781978539556 (paperback) | ISBN 9781978539570 (ebook)
Subjects: LCSH: Air Force One (Presidential aircraft)–Juvenile literature. | Presidents–Transportation–United States–Juvenile literature.
Classification: LCC TL723 .B73 2025 | DDC 387.7/42088352230973–dc23/eng/20240131
LC record available at https://lccn.loc.gov/2023059777

Published in 2025 by
Enslow Publishing
2544 Clinton Street
Buffalo, NY 14224

Portions of this work were originally authored by Ryan Nagelhout and published as *Air Force One*. All new material in this edition is authored by Eleanor Bradshaw.

Designer: Andrea Davison-Bartolotta
Editor: Rachael Morlock

Photo credits: Cover Photo by Airman 1st Class Daniel Hughes/Nellis AFB Public Affairs/DVIDS; series art (metal background texture) caesart/Shutterstock.com; series art (title font) TortugaStudios/Shutterstock.com; p. 5 Florida Chuck/Shutterstock.com; p. 7 courtesy of National Archives; p. 8 U.S. Air Force photo/National Museum of the United States Air Force; p. 9 https://en.wikipedia.org/wiki/File:Lyndon_B._Johnson_taking_the_oath_of_office,_November_1963.jpg/Wikimedia Commons; p. 10 Andreas Stroh/Shutterstock.com; p. 11 Photo by Senior Airman Ashlyn Correia/157th Air Refueling Wing/DVIDS; p. 13 aurielaki/Shutterstock.com; p. 15 U.S. Air Force photo/Master Sgt. Jim Varhegyi; p. 17 Photo by Staff Sgt. Jarad Denton/501st Combat Support Wing Public Affairs/DVIDS; p. 18 Photo by Senior Airman John Pharr/129th Rescue Wing/DVIDS; p. 19 Photo by Senior Airman Brittany Chase/35th Fighter Wing Public Affairs/DVIDS; p. 20 Jason Schronce/Shutterstock.com; p. 21 The White House/Flickr.

Printed in the United States of America

CPSIA compliance information: Batch #CS25ENS: For further information contact Enslow Publishing, at 1-800-398-2504.

CONTENTS

Boldface words appear in Words to Know.

THE PRESIDENT'S PLANE

At any time, a **military** plane is ready to fly the U.S. president where they need to go! Any U.S. **air force** plane the president rides on is called Air Force One during the flight. But some planes have been specially made for the president to use.

This plane was made to fly the president of the United States around the country and the world.

FIRST PRESIDENTIAL FLIGHTS

During **World War II**, air travel became an important way to **transport** the president. The air force used a plane called the "**Sacred Cow**" for President Franklin D. Roosevelt. It had a sleeping area, radio telephone, and elevator for the president's wheelchair.

In 1943, Roosevelt (left) became the first president to fly in an airplane while in office.

In the early 1960s, presidential planes became known as Air Force One. A plane was specially **designed** for President John F. Kennedy in 1962. Another was built in 1972. Two new jets replaced them in 1990 and 1991. They are still used today!

President Kennedy was killed in Dallas, Texas, on November 22, 1963. Just hours later, Lyndon B. Johnson (center) became president aboard Air Force One.

SPECIAL JETS

Today's Air Force One planes are two Boeing 747-200B jets. Each jet is white with a blue nose. "United States of America" is written on the side. The presidential seal is on the nose, and an American flag is on the tail.

PRESIDENTIAL SEAL

The Air Force One jets are as long as a city block and as tall as a six-story building.

BUILT FOR BUSINESS

Each Air Force One jet is made up of three decks. **Passengers** use the rooms on the middle deck. These rooms include offices, a meeting room, and a medical center. The president also has a **private** bedroom, bathroom, and office.

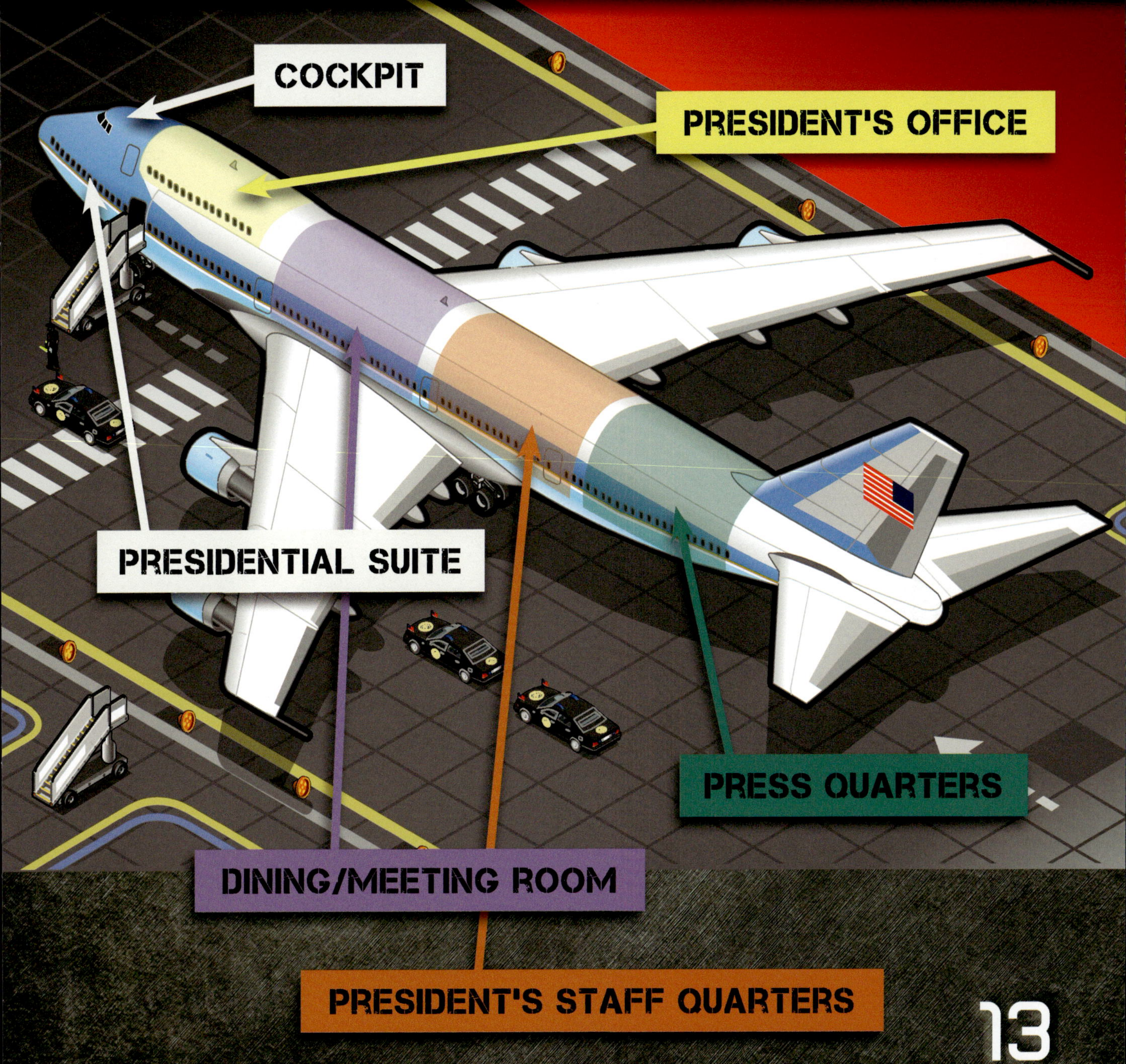
COCKPIT
PRESIDENT'S OFFICE
PRESIDENTIAL SUITE
PRESS QUARTERS
DINING/MEETING ROOM
PRESIDENT'S STAFF QUARTERS

A FULL FLIGHT

Passengers often include the president's staff and family, the vice president, government officials, and members of the press. The crew prepares food for everyone in two kitchens. The plane always has 2,000 meals on hand, and 100 people can eat at a time.

Special training is needed to be part of the Air Force One crew.

READY FOR TAKEOFF

Air Force One can't land at the White House. Instead, a helicopter brings the president from the White House to Andrews Air Force Base in Maryland. Air Force One takes off from there! Other air force planes fly ahead and behind Air Force One wherever it goes.

Any Marine Corps helicopter the president rides in is called Marine One.

SAFE TRAVELS

Air Force One is very safe. It's made of special strong glass and metal to guard the president from **attack**. It can **refuel** in the air in case it can't land. Some parts of Air Force One are top secret.

Air Force One's flight crew and staff are all members of the U.S. Air Force.

ON THE MOVE

Air Force One has an important job to do! It gives the president a place to work and rest while in the air. The president trusts the plane and its crew to fly safely around the country and the world.

This picture shows President Joe Biden working aboard Air Force One!

WORDS TO KNOW

air force: The branch of the military that works with planes and helicopters.

attack: To try to harm someone or something.

design: To create the pattern or shape of something.

military: Relating to the armed services.

passenger: Someone who rides on a plane, car, or bus.

private: Belonging to one person.

refuel: To add fuel to.

sacred: Holy or deserving of honor.

transport: To move people or things from one place to another.

World War II: A war fought from 1939 to 1945 that involved countries around the world.

FOR MORE INFORMATION

BOOKS

Duling, Kaitlyn. *Air Force One: Protecting the President's Plane.* North Mankato, MN: Capstone Press, 2020.

Garstecki, Julia. *U.S. Air Force.* Mankato, MN: Black Rabbit Books, 2021.

WEBSITES

Air Force One

www.whitehouse.gov/about-the-white-house/the-grounds/air-force-one/

Find facts about the president's "office in the sky" on the White House website.

How Air Force One Works

people.howstuffworks.com/air-force-one.htm

Learn more about what's inside Air Force One.

INDEX